W9-AYE-153

AWESOME SUPER SIMPLE
HABITAT PROJECTS

SUPER SIMPLE

OCEAN

PROJECTS

FUN & EASY ANIMAL ENVIRONMENT ACTIVITIES

CAROLYN BERNHARDT

CONSULTING EDITOR, DIANE CRAIG, M.A./READING SPECIALIST

Super Sandcastle

An Imprint of Abdo Publishing
abdopublishing.com

abdopublishing.com

Published by Abdo Publishing, a division of ABDO, PO Box 398166, Minneapolis, Minnesota 55439. Copyright © 2017 by Abdo Consulting Group, Inc. International copyrights reserved in all countries. No part of this book may be reproduced in any form without written permission from the publisher. Super SandCastle™ is a trademark and logo of Abdo Publishing.

Printed in the United States of America, North Mankato, Minnesota
102016
012017

THIS BOOK CONTAINS
RECYCLED MATERIALS

Editor: Liz Salzmann
Content Developer: Nancy Tuminelly
Cover and Interior Design and Production: Mighty Media, Inc.
Photo Credits: AP Images; Mighty Media, Inc.; Shutterstock

The following manufacturers/names appearing in this book are trademarks: Craft Smart®, Jell-O®, Morton®, Pyrex®, Scotch®, Sharpie®

Publisher's Cataloging-in-Publication Data

Names: Bernhardt, Carolyn, author.
Title: Super simple ocean projects: fun & easy animal environment activities / by Carolyn Bernhardt.
Other titles: Fun & easy animal environment activities | Fun and easy animal environment activities
Description: Minneapolis, MN : Abdo Publishing, 2017. | Series: Awesome super simple habitat projects
Identifiers: LCCN 2016944669 | ISBN 9781680784428 (lib. bdg.) | ISBN 9781680797954 (ebook)
Subjects: LCSH: Habitats--Juvenile literature. | Habitat (Ecology)--Juvenile literature. | Ocean ecology--Juvenile literature.
Classification: DDC 577.7--dc23
LC record available at http://lccn.loc.gov/2016944669

Super SandCastle™ books are created by a team of professional educators, reading specialists, and content developers around five essential components—phonemic awareness, phonics, vocabulary, text comprehension, and fluency—to assist young readers as they develop reading skills and strategies and increase their general knowledge. All books are written, reviewed, and leveled for guided reading, early reading intervention, and Accelerated Reader™ programs for use in shared, guided, and independent reading and writing activities to support a balanced approach to literacy instruction.

To Adult Helpers

The projects in this book are fun and simple. There are just a few things to remember to keep kids safe. Some projects require the use of sharp or hot objects. Also, kids may be using messy materials such as glue or paint. Make sure they protect their clothes and work surfaces. Review the projects before starting, and be ready to assist when necessary.

....

KEY SYMBOLS

Watch for these warning symbols in this book. Here is what they mean.

HOT!
You will be working with something hot. Get help!

SHARP!
You will be working with a sharp object. Get help!

CONTENTS

OVERFLOWING
OCEANS

Water covers more than 70 percent of Earth! Most of this water is in the world's oceans. Temperature and **depth** is different in every ocean. But all oceans support many kinds of animals and plants!

Do you know how old the ocean is? Scientists believe there were living organisms in the ocean more than 3 **billion** years ago. Oceans support more life than just the creatures that live in their waters. People and land animals use oceans for food, water, and **transportation**!

FOOD FROM THE OCEAN

TRANSPORTATION ON THE OCEAN

THE WORLD OCEAN

There are five oceans. They are the Arctic Ocean, the Atlantic Ocean, the Pacific Ocean, the Indian Ocean, and the Southern Ocean. All of the oceans are connected. Together, they make up the World Ocean.

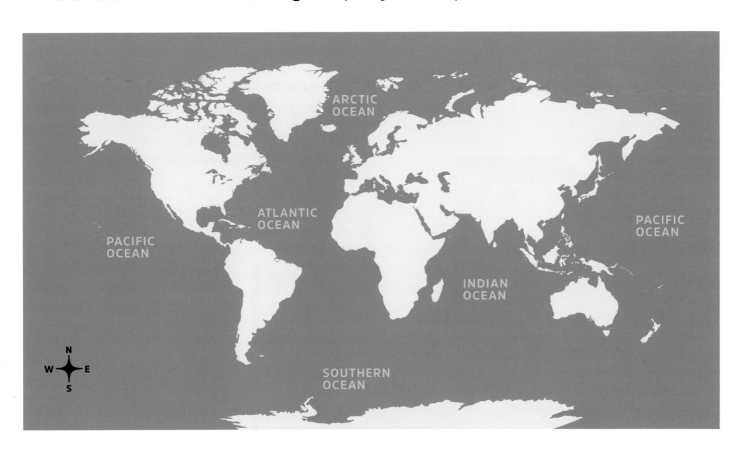

OCEAN
WILDLIFE

The world's oceans are home to many animals! This includes fish, crabs, whales, dolphins, and more. Different animals live in different oceans. They go where the conditions provide what they need to survive.

WALRUSES

Walruses are often found in the icy waters of the Arctic Ocean. A walrus has a thick layer of fat under its skin. It is called blubber. The blubber keeps the walrus warm in cold water.

Manatees live in the warmer southern Atlantic Ocean. A manatee doesn't have a layer of fat to keep it warm. This is one reason it needs to live in warm water.

MANATEE

MELTING ICE BREAKING OFF INTO THE OCEAN

CLIMATE CHANGE

A huge amount of water is stored as ice in the Arctic and in Antarctica. Scientists have observed that **climate change** is causing this ice to melt. The water from the melting ice goes into the ocean. This causes the water level around the world to rise. The water temperature changes too. These changes can affect all the creatures in the ocean.

HABITAT
FOOD CHAIN

Every natural **habitat** has a food chain. The food chain shows what each animal eats. When humans harm a habitat, they ruin the food chain's balance. This causes some animals to go hungry.

OCEAN FOOD CHAIN

A food chain has several levels. The animals in one level mostly eat the animals in the level below. But some animals can be on more than one level.

The bottom, or level 1, of a food chain is plants. They make their own food from sunlight, air, and water. Level 2 of a food chain is **herbivores**. Level 3 is **carnivores** that eat herbivores. Level 4 is the top of a food chain. This level is carnivores that eat other carnivores. These animals have few predators.

4

3

2

1

LEVEL 1

OCEAN PLANTS

algae, kelp, **phytoplankton**, seaweed

CLARK AND SHARKS

Eugenie Clark was interested in fish, especially sharks. She showed people how beautiful and important sharks are. Clark was one of the first people to use **scuba** gear to study sea creatures. She discovered many new **species** of fish. Clark helped teach the world how special the ocean is. Her discoveries greatly improved ocean science.

— LEVEL 2 —

OCEAN HERBIVORES

manatees, mussels, oysters, sea urchins, shrimps

— LEVEL 3 —

OCEAN CARNIVORES

blue crabs, humpback whales, lobsters, octopuses, penguins, seals

— LEVEL 4 —

OCEAN CARNIVORES

dolphins, killer whales, marlins, sharks, tuna

MATERIALS

Here are some of the materials that you will need for the projects in this book.

ALUMINUM PAN   CARD STOCK   CELLOPHANE SHEETS   CHENILLE STEMS   CLAY   CONSTRUCTION PAPER

CRAFT FOAM   CRAFT STICKS   DOUBLE-SIDED TAPE   EYEDROPPER   FLORAL FOAM   FOOD COLORING

GELATIN POWDER

GLASS BAKING DISH

GOOGLY EYES

LONG KNIFE

MATCHES

MEASURING CUP

MEASURING
SPOONS

PAINT

PAINTBRUSH

PERMANENT
MARKER

PIE PAN

PLASTIC CONTAINER

RULER

SALT

SHOE BOX

STYROFOAM BALLS

TEA CANDLE

TOOTHPICK

OCEAN ZONES

MATERIALS: set of 5 clear stacking jars, water, food coloring (yellow, blue & purple), craft stick, scissors, card stock, marker, tape

The ocean has five main layers, called zones. Each zone gets a different amount of sunlight. This depends on how deep the water is. Sunlight can't reach the deepest parts of the ocean. It is completely dark there. As the ocean gets shallower, it becomes lighter. From deepest to shallowest, the ocean zones are trench, abyss, midnight, twilight, and sunlight.

MAKE A STACK OF OCEAN COLORS!

① Fill each of the jars with water.

② Add one drop of yellow food coloring to one jar. Add one drop of blue coloring to the second jar. Add two drops of blue coloring to the third jar. Add three drops of blue coloring to the fourth jar. Add three drops of blue coloring and one drop of purple coloring to the fifth jar.

③ Stir the water in the jars with a craft stick.

④ **Stack** the jars with the lightest one on top.

⑤ Cut a piece of card stock as tall as the stacked jars. Divide the card into five sections. Write the ocean zones in the sections.

⑥ Tape the card to the stack of jars. Make sure each label lines up with the correct jar.

TREMENDOUS TIPPY
TIDE POOL

MATERIALS: aluminum pan, sand, rocks, pebbles, seashells, plastic sea animals, water

Tide pools are located on the ocean shore. They are underwater during high tide. At low tide, these pools have shallow water. Some tide pools dry up during low tide. So, animals in tide pools live part of the time underwater. But part of the time they are out of the water. This means they have to adapt to different surroundings.

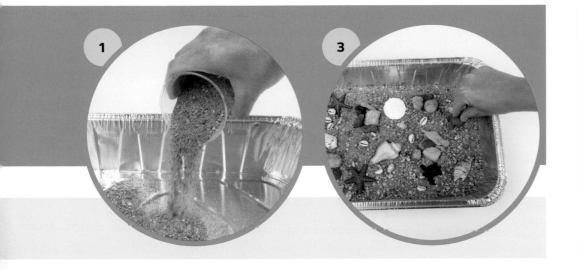

CREATE A TIDE POOL!

① Cover the bottom of the pan with sand.

② Add rocks, pebbles, and seashells.

③ Add plastic sea animals.

④ Carefully pour water into the pan. Add enough water to cover the rocks.

⑤ Gently tip the tide pool from side to side. Watch the animals go from sea creatures to land dwellers!

DIGGING DEEPER

The water protects ocean creatures from getting too much sun. But animals in tide pools don't always have the cover of water. So, they find other ways to get protection from the sun. **Sea anemones** cover up in bits of shell. Hermit crabs find seashells to live in. These animals can stay safe in all tide levels!

CORAL REEF CLUSTER

MATERIALS: blue paint, paintbrush, shoe box, long knife, floral foam, ruler, green construction paper, scissors, craft foam, glue, googly eyes, double-sided tape, chenille stems, Styrofoam balls

Coral is hard and sharp, so it seems like a type of rock. But coral is the skeleton of a sea animal called a coral polyp. Polyps attach themselves to rocks or other underwater objects. Then they grow into large formations called coral **reefs**. Coral reefs give lots of undersea life a safe place to hide from predators.

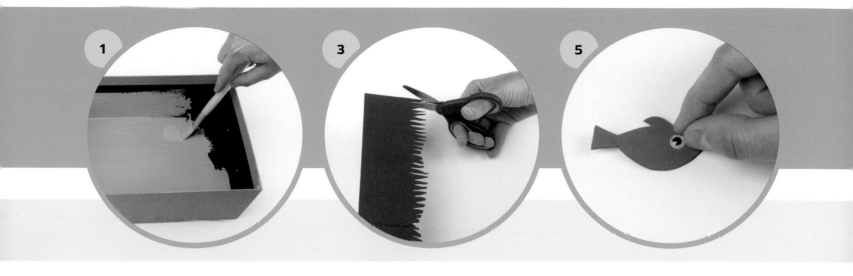

MAKE A CORAL REEF SHADOWBOX!

1. Paint the inside of the box blue. Let it dry.

2. With adult help, cut the floral foam. Cut a piece the size of a long side of the box. Make it 2 inches (5 cm) thick.

3. Cut a strip of green construction paper as long as the floral foam piece. Make it 2½ inches (6 cm) wide. Cut grass blades along a long side.

4. With adult help, **research** coral and the animals that live in coral **reefs**.

5. Cut sea creatures out of craft foam. Glue on googly eyes.

Continued on the next page.

CORAL REEF CLUSTER (CONTINUED)

⑥ Set the box on its side. Place the floral foam in the box. Stick the grass to the foam with double-sided tape.

⑦ Tape some sea creatures to the inside of the box. Glue others to the floral foam.

⑧ Cut pieces of chenille stem. Wrap them around each into an antler shape. Leave a stem sticking down. This is a staghorn coral.

⑨ Push the bottom stem into the floral foam.

⑩ Cut a Styrofoam ball in half. Wrap chenille stems into small circles. Glue them to the rounded surface of each half of the ball. These are star corals.

⑪ Glue the flat sides of the star corals to the floral foam.

DIGGING DEEPER

Coral **reefs** are in danger from overfishing and pollution. Fish are important for coral reefs to survive. They eat the **algae** off of coral reefs. This keeps coral reefs healthy and clean. So, removing too many fish harms coral reefs. Coral reefs need clean water. Pollution from cities, factories, cars, and farms causes harmful changes to ocean water. Changes to the water's **depth**, temperature, and clearness make it difficult for coral to survive and grow.

CITIES

FACTORIES

CARS AND TRUCKS

FARMING

OVERFISHING

UNEXPLORED UNDERSEA

MATERIALS: small box of gelatin powder, pie pan, 2-cup measuring cup, water, ice cubes, spoon, refrigerator, tablespoons, clay, permanent marker, notebook, pencil, scissors, colored paper, toothpicks, glue

The ocean affects and supports all life on Earth in one way or another. But less than 5 percent of the ocean has been explored. Imagine all of the life we have not yet found. The possibilities are endless!

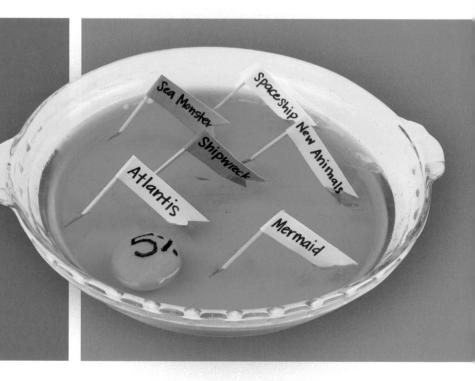

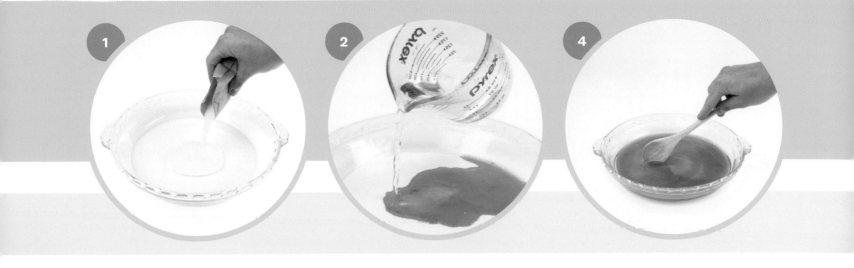

MAKE YOUR OWN OCEAN!

1 Put the gelatin powder in the pie pan.

2 Boil ¾ cup of water. Pour it into the pie pan.

3 Put ½ cup of water in the measuring cup. Add ice cubes until the water measures 1¼ cups.

4 Pour the ice water into the pie pan. Stir the mixture until it starts getting thick. Remove any remaining pieces of ice.

5 Put the pie pan in the refrigerator. Leave it there until the gelatin is completely firm. This takes about one hour.

6 The pie pan contains 2 cups of gelatin. This represents the ocean.

Continued on the next page.

UNEXPLORED UNDERSEA (CONTINUED)

⑦ Measure 1½ tablespoons of clay. This is 5 percent of 2 cups. It represents the explored portion of the ocean.

⑧ Roll the clay into a ball. Label it "5%" with the marker.

⑨ Place the ball of clay on the gelatin.

⑩ Think about what might be in the unexplored 95 percent of the ocean. Write your ideas in a notebook.

⑪ Cut strips of colored paper. Fold them in half. Cut a triangle into the open end of each folded strip. Write one of your ideas on each strip.

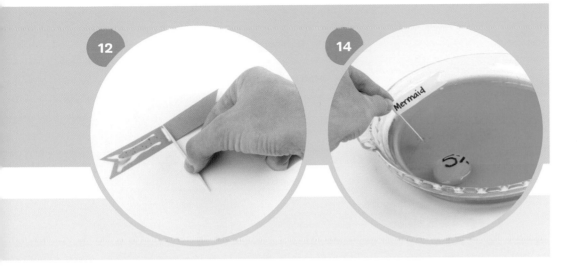

12 Unfold a strip. Place a toothpick on the fold. Put glue on one side of the strip. Fold the strip around the toothpick to make a flag.

13 Repeat step 12 with the other strips of paper.

14 Stick the flags into the gelatin.

15 Show your friends and family what you think might be in the unexplored ocean!

DIGGING DEEPER

There are many unsolved mysteries in the ocean. Less than 1 percent of the ocean floor has been mapped. Scientists use special tools to measure the ocean floor. However, the tools can't reach the deepest parts of the ocean. What do you think they would find if they could go deeper?

CANDLE CURRENT

CURRENT

MATERIALS: 2 glass cups, glass baking dish, small glass bowl, tea candle, spoon, salt, water, craft foam, scissors, match, blue food coloring

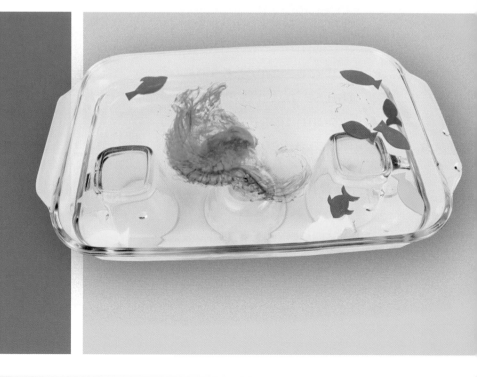

The ocean has currents. Currents are streams of water flowing below the surface. Currents can move in many different directions.

Differences in water temperature can cause a current. Warm water moves differently than cold water. So when cold and warm water meet, they push against each other. This causes the water to move in a current.

MAKE A VISIBLE OCEAN CURRENT!

① Place the cups on a table. Set the baking dish on top of the cups. The cups should be evenly spaced to balance the dish.

② Place the small bowl upside down between the cups. Set the candle on the bowl.

③ Put a spoonful of salt in the baking dish.

④ Fill the dish three-fourths full of water. Stir well.

⑤ Cut fish shapes out of craft foam. Put them in the water.

⑥ Have an adult help you light the candle. The flame heats the water, creating a current. Watch as the fish start to move!

⑦ Add a drop of blue food coloring to reveal the current.

ARCTIC OCEAN
SEA ICE

MATERIALS: plastic sea animals, plastic container, water, freezer, dish towel, glass bowl, eyedropper

Sea ice is frozen seawater. There is a lot of sea ice in the Arctic Ocean. Sea ice forms in pieces. Large pieces of sea ice are called ice floes. They can be more than 6 miles (10 km) across. Many creatures live near and on sea ice.

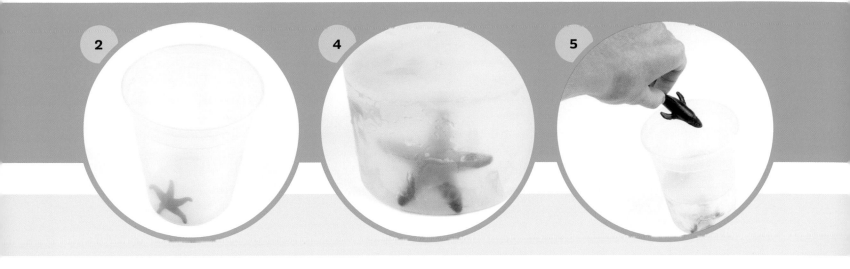

CREATE AN ICY ARCTIC HABITAT!

(1) **With adult help, research** the animals that live in the Arctic Ocean. Then gather plastic arctic sea animals.

(2) Place the animals that live on the floor of the Arctic Ocean in the plastic container.

(3) Pour water into the container until the animals are covered.

(4) Place the container in the freezer. Remove it when the water is frozen solid.

(5) Place the animals that swim higher in the Arctic Ocean in the container. Cover the animals with water.

Continued on the next page.

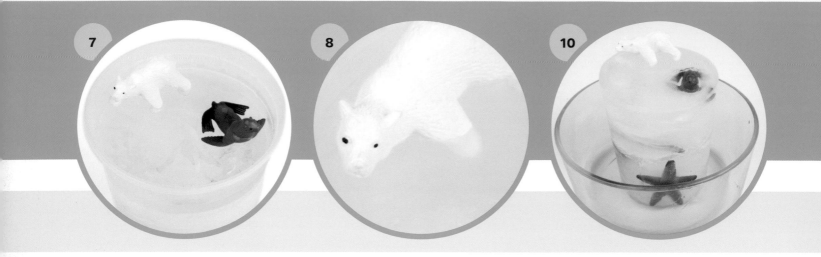

ARCTIC OCEAN SEA ICE (CONTINUED)

⑥ Freeze this layer until it is solid.

⑦ Place animals that live on sea ice in the container. Add just enough water to cover their feet.

⑧ Place the container back in the freezer.

Make sure the animals are standing or sitting up. When the water freezes, it will keep them upright.

⑨ Remove the container from the freezer. Get a dish **towel** wet with warm water. Hold the towel around the container so the ice melts slightly. Repeat this until the ice moves freely in the container.

⑩ Carefully remove the ice from the container. Place it in the bowl.

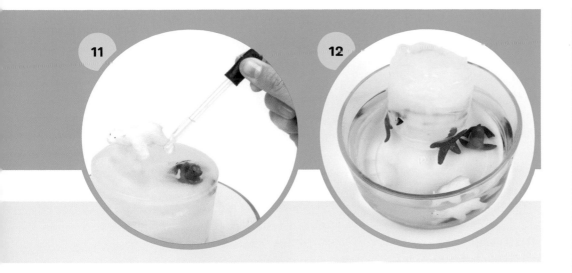

11 Use the eyedropper to drop water onto the ice. Repeat until the ice starts to melt before your eyes!

12 Watch as the ice melts away. This is what **climate change** is doing to the world's sea ice. How are the animals in your ice affected?

DIGGING DEEPER

The Arctic is a very hard place to live on Earth. It has many strong snowstorms. The sun never shines there during winter months. But the Arctic is still packed with wildlife. Animals such as polar bears, arctic hares, and walruses have learned how to survive these conditions. These animals need the ice to live. Their **habitat** is disappearing with the sea ice.

CONCLUSION

The ocean covers most of our planet. It is home to a lot of wildlife. It also helps support humans and other land animals. This book is the first step in learning more about the ocean and how to protect it. There is so much more to find out!

Do you live near an ocean? Have you ever visited one? Go to the library to **research** the world's oceans. Or have an adult help you research oceans **online**. Learn about what you can do to help preserve the oceans!

QUIZ

(1) How many oceans make up the World Ocean?

(2) Do manatees live in warm or cold water?

(3) Coral **reefs** are made of plants.
TRUE OR FALSE?

THINK ABOUT IT!

What would the world be like if there were no oceans?

GLOSSARY

algae – a plant or plantlike organism that lives in water.

billion – a very large number. One billion is also written 1,000,000,000.

carnivore – an animal that eats mainly meat.

climate change – a long-term change in Earth's climate.

depth – how deep something is.

habitat – the area or environment where a person or animal usually lives.

herbivore – an animal that eats mainly plants.

online – connected to the Internet.

phytoplankton – tiny plant life in bodies of water.

reef – a strip of coral, rock, or sand that is near the surface of the ocean.

research – to find out more about something.

scuba – a system that lets swimmers breathe underwater using a tank of air.

sea anemone – a small, brightly colored sea animal that looks like a flower and sticks to things such as rocks and coral.

species – a group of related living beings.

stack – 1. a pile of things placed one on top of the other. 2. to put things on top of each other.

towel – a cloth or paper used for cleaning or drying.

transportation – the act of moving people and things.

Book Due Latest Date Shown